Wing Strokes Haiku

Wing Strokes Haiku

by

Sydell Rosenberg & Amy Losak

Cover by Shay Culligan
Cover art by Zac Ong from Unsplash

ISBN: 978-1-63980-107-7

Kelsay Books
502 South 1040 East, A-119
American Fork, Utah 84003
Kelsaybooks.com

To everyone I love in my life: my husband Cliff, family, friends, and colleagues. Thank you for your ongoing encouragement. I could not have done this without you.

brooding
over world events
cicadas

First Place, 2021 Haiku Society of America Senryu Award
in Memorial of Gerald Brady

Acknowledgments

A number of the poems in this book first appeared in the following:

Akitsu Quarterly
American Haiku
Asahi Haikuist Network
The Daily Haiku
Frogpond
Haiga Online
Haiku Chronicles
Haiku Commentary
The Haiku Foundation
Haiku Magazine
Haiku Newton
Haiku Poets of the Garden State/New Jersey Botanical Garden
Haiku Zasshi Zo
Hedgerow
The Heron's Nest
Holden Arboretum Haiku Path
Janus & SCTH
The Living Haiku Anthology
Prune Juice
Tinywords
Under the Basho

Contents

shinning up the stem
  beetle confronts butterfly
    sated with nectar   ~SR

forsythia bush
  chirping
    yellow   ~AL

a mad struggle out—
   the moth searches for a place
      where his wings can grow   ~SR

sun-clock
   my day unwinds with
      low-flying sparrows   ~AL

standing in the rain
  two tree trunks tied together
    by a spider's web   ~SR

on the wings
  of starlings ...
    morning moon   ~AL

one-winged butterfly
   still beating
      at the sky   ~SR

midtown fountain
   a dancer pirouettes
      with a pigeon   ~AL

warning his mother
to walk softly...
a butterfly   ~SR

life lesson—
the pinwheel call
of a cardinal   ~AL

the autumn leaves lie
  like moth-eaten applique
    on the velvet green   ~SR

city book stalls
  invisible birds
    peeping poems   ~AL

like that butterfly
   I sail through holes in the fence
      made of woven wire   ~SR

luring me
   to a lambent lake…
      the loon's lullaby   ~AL

arranging his wares
  the Creepy Crawly vendor
    sends a spider up   ~SR

under a cold sun
  mourning doves cheerily coo
    in spite of it all   ~AL

bathroom cleaning
  a dirt speck
    sprouts legs   ~AL

airless summer days
  iridescence the silver throat
    of my tea kettle   ~SR

as darkness descends
　　the young black cat makes a toy
　　　of a mosquito　　　~AL

a flock of pigeons
　　swoops into one giant wing
　　　in the sharp blue sky　　　~SR

sodden Saturday...
   worms curling into letters
      on a sidewalk square   ~AL

"Guaranteed to Sing!"
   she brings home a canary
      to an empty room   ~SR

warming up the seat
  dots of white, like fireflies
    shimmer in the beams   ~AL

freezing morning
  a giant squeeze toy full of
    grackles and pigeons   ~SR

pink pagodas
  a plump bee waggles
    in a primrose   ~AL

in their deep nest
  the young reed warblers wait
    gasping with the heat   ~SR

spider
　in a web
　　trapping stars　　~AL

in a toyless cage
　the parakeet discovers
　　a feather to twirl　　~SR

rising and falling
  with every breath…
    ladybug   ~AL

caught in the act—
  a sparrow with a bread cube
    in his vise-like beak   ~SR

neighbor's yard
   three brown butterflies
      braid the air   ~AL

after the downpour
  squawks of a blue jay
     heavy on a branch   ~SR

capering
　on a sycamore pillar—
　　caterpillar　　　~AL

eleven wild swans
　cut their flight in mid-ocean
　　to rest on a rock　　　~SR

suburban street fair
  a yellow swallowtail
    hugs a sugar stick   ~AL

hummingbird's wings
  defying
    the camera   ~SR

stuck inside
  I make friends
    with a stinkbug   ~AL

wildfires—
  a seagull
    howls at the sun   ~AL

rupturing my rest
  the rhythmic rasp
    of a cricket   ~AL

post-layoff surprise
  the sweeter sound
    of birdsong   ~AL

after a journey
   the cobwebs that confront me
     are not my doing   ~SR

plucked from her own breast
   the mallard duck makes her nest
     on a dank piling   ~SR

hazy summer day
  only yellow school buses
    and white butterflies   ~SR

feathers fall mutely
  to the bottom of a cage
    like white rose petals   ~SR

About the Authors

Amy Losak spent most of her life in Queens, New York, and now lives in New Jersey. She is a healthcare public relations consultant. Her mother, Sydell Rosenberg, was a teacher and published writer, especially poetry—primarily haiku and related forms. Syd was a charter member of the Haiku Society of America in 1968. Amy is a member today.

Syd, who died in 1996, contributed to the literary life of her home borough and New York City. Her "city haiku" and other poems were published in leading journals, classic anthologies (such as *The Haiku Anthology* and *The Haiku Handbook: How to Write, Share, and Teach Haiku),* and other media dedicated to this luminous form. In 1994, Syd's senryu was featured in the New York public arts project, *Haiku on 42nd Street,* in which old theater marquees in Times Square were transformed into "frames" for short poems.

Thanks to Syd's influence, Amy writes and publishes her own haiku today. Her credits include *Akitsu Quarterly, Autumn Moon Haiku Journal, Failed Haiku, Frameless Sky, Frogpond* (the journal of HSA)*, The Haiku Foundation, Hedgerow The Heron's Nest, Modern Haiku, Newtown Literary, Prune Juice, Tinywords;* and more, including several anthologies.

In 2018, Penny Candy Books, started by two poets, released *H Is For Haiku* (illustrated by Sawsan Chalabi). Amy wrote the introduction. This vibrant children's collection was honored by the National Council for Teachers of English as a 2019 "Notable Poetry Book."

In 2020, the respected independent literary publisher, Kattywompus Press, released Syd's chapbook for adults, *Poised Across the Sky*. Amy and founder Sammy Greenspan served as co-editors.

Amy also is a member of The Bookniks (formerly The Book Meshuggenahs), a group of female Jewish authors in the United States and Israel. They write children's books and serve as a resource for the Jewish community.